MARTIN LUTHER KING JR.

MARTIN LUTHER KING JR.

WALKING IN THE LIGHT

JON M. FISHMAN

LERNER PUBLICATIONS ◆ MINNEAPOLIS

Lerner Publications Company
A division of Lerner Publishing Group, Inc.
241 First Avenue North
Minneapolis, MN USA 55401

For reading levels and more information, look up this title at www.lernerbooks.com.

Image credits: Howard Sochurek/The LIFE Picture Collection/Getty Images, p. 2; Francis Miller/ The LIFE Picture Collection/Getty Images, p. 6; Marion S. Trikosko/Library of Congress (LC-DIG-ds-04000), p. 8; Robert W. Kelley/The LIFE Picture Collection/Getty Images, p. 9; PhotoQuest/ Getty Images, p. 10; Bettmann/Getty Images, pp. 11, 24, 28, 31, 39; Jet Lowe/Library of Congress (HABS GA,61-ATLA,54--2), p. 12; CSU Archives/Everett Collection/Newscom, p. 13; John Vachon/Library of Congress (LC-DIG-fsa-8a03228), p. 14; Jack Delano/Library of Congress (LC-DIG-ppmsc-00199), p. 15; John van Hasselt/Sygma/Getty Images, p. 16; Al Moldvay/The Denver Post/Getty Images, p. 17; Ann Ronan Pictures/Hulton Archive/Getty Images, p. 19; Michael Ochs Archives/Getty Images, p. 20; Universal History Archive/UIG/Getty images, p. 22; Don Cravens/ The LIFE Images Collection/Getty Images, pp. 23, 25, 26, 27, 29; AP Photo/R. Satakopan, p. 30; Donald Uhrbrock/The LIFE Images Collection/Getty Images, p. 32; Paul Schutzer/The LIFE Picture Collection/Getty Images, pp. 33, 34; AP Photo, pp. 35, 38; Lyndon Baines Johnson Library photo by Cecil Stoughton, p. 37; Stephen F. Somerstein/Archive Photos/Getty Images, p. 41.

Cover: Archive Photos/Getty Images.

Main body text set in Rotis Serif Std 55 Regular 13.5/17. Typeface provided by Adobe Systems.

Library of Congress Cataloging-in-Publication Data

Names: Fishman, Jon M., author.
Title: Martin Luther King Jr.: walking in the light / Jon M. Fishman.
Description: Minneapolis: Lerner Publications, [2019] | Series: Gateway biographies | Includes
    bibliographical references and index. | Audience: Grades 4–6. | Audience: Ages 9–14.
Identifiers: LCCN 2018026949 (print) | LCCN 2018029301 (ebook) | ISBN 9781541543485
    (eb pdf) | ISBN 9781541539181 (lb : alk. paper)
Subjects: LCSH: King, Martin Luther, Jr., 1929-1968–Juvenile literature. | African Americans–
    Biography–Juvenile literature. | Civil rights workers–United States–Biography–Juvenile
    literature. | African Americans–Civil rights–History–20th century–Juvenile literature. | Civil
    rights movements–United States–History–20th century–Juvenile literature. | Nonviolence–
    United States–History–20th century–Juvenile literature.
Classification: LCC E185.97.K5 (ebook) | LCC E185.97.K5 F495 2019 (print) | DDC 323.092 [B]
    —dc23

LC record available at https://lccn.loc.gov/2018026949

Manufactured in the United States of America
1-45101-35928-9/11/2018

CONTENTS

Martin Luther King Jr. speaks to demonstrators in Chicago in 1960.

About 250,000 people gathered in front of the Washington Monument in Washington, DC, on August 28, 1963. The huge crowd included people of different ages, races, and social classes. They were participating in the March on Washington for Jobs and Freedom. Some carried signs demanding equal rights and better job opportunities for all US citizens. Others called for an end to racial segregation that kept black people and white people apart in places such as schools and restaurants. As the crowd marched down the National Mall toward the Lincoln Memorial, many held hands or linked arms with those around them.

Plans for the March on Washington had been underway for months. It was part of the civil rights movement, the fight in the 1950s and 1960s to end discrimination and segregation in the United States. Leaders of the movement came together to raise money for transportation and to recruit marchers. They hoped about one hundred thousand people would attend the march, but

About 250,000 people participated in the 1963 March on Washington.

more than twice as many people showed up that day.

The crowd that assembled in front of the Lincoln Memorial stretched down both sides of the Lincoln Memorial Reflecting Pool. The tightly packed gathering made the pleasant day feel hot and muggy. People fanned themselves and even dipped their feet into the pool to cool off as speakers such as John Lewis, a civil rights leader and future member of the US Congress, took turns addressing the crowd.

The final speaker of the day was Martin Luther King Jr., a Baptist pastor and prominent leader of the civil rights movement. Reading a speech he had prepared in advance, King spoke of the country's long history of racial injustice. He reminded the crowd that although Abraham Lincoln's Emancipation Proclamation had ended legal slavery in the United States more than one hundred years earlier, black people still were not free of racial segregation and bias.

King was known for his ability to excite and inspire people with his words. Yet as his speech at the March on Washington went on, some felt it wasn't having much

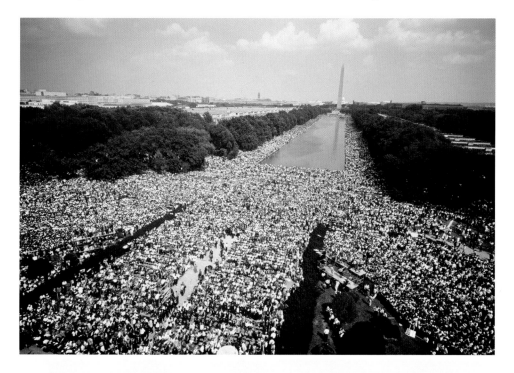

Demonstrators filled the National Mall during the March on Washington. This image shows the Washington Monument on the far side of the reflecting pool.

of an impact on the crowd. Perhaps everyone was worn down after a long, hot day of marching and listening to speeches. Gospel singer Mahalia Jackson, who stood near King during the event, called out to him. She told him to stop reading his speech and instead to speak from the heart as he had done so many times in the past.

Speaking without his prepared words, King talked about his dreams of equality and freedom. He encouraged

King speaks to the crowd from the steps of the Lincoln Memorial.

When King began talking about his dreams instead of delivering his prepared speech, the energy of the crowd picked up.

people from all social classes and all races to come together to make the United States better. He spoke of his vision that someday in this country skin color wouldn't determine where you could work or eat.

King's speech stirred the crowd and the nation. His words, especially those that he hadn't written, became one of the most celebrated speeches in US history and of the civil rights movement. Author James Baldwin, who was at the March on Washington that day, said he could feel the crowd's passion for King's words. "It almost seemed that we stood on a height, and could see our inheritance; perhaps we could make the kingdom real," Baldwin wrote.

Ebenezer Baptist Church in Atlanta, Georgia, where Martin's father was a pastor

SOUTHERN HERITAGE

Martin Luther King Jr. was born on January 15, 1929, in his family's home on Auburn Avenue in Atlanta, Georgia. His father, Martin Luther King Sr., was a pastor at Atlanta's Ebenezer Baptist Church. He had taken over the job from Martin's grandfather, Adam Daniel Williams, in 1931.

Martin was an active and curious child. He liked sports, especially football and baseball. His mother, Alberta King, taught him to play the piano and read before Martin was old enough to go to school. His home was a happy place where he received love and kindness, and his family experience gave Martin a friendly attitude toward people and the world.

From an early age, Martin displayed a special sensitivity about some of the problems society faced. He was born near the beginning of the Great Depression (1929–1939), when banks failed and the US economy declined. Millions of Americans couldn't find work and struggled to survive. When he was about five years old, Martin observed breadlines in Atlanta—long lines of desperate people waiting to receive free food. The experience taught him that even in a wealthy country like the United States, some people needed help to pay for food, clothing, and shelter.

Martin also learned about racism. His mother explained to him that black people had been slaves in parts of North America for hundreds of years. In the United States, slavery officially became illegal

Martin with his family. *Top row, from left:* mother, Alberta Williams King; father, Martin Luther King Sr.; and grandmother, Jennie Williams. *Bottom row, from left:* brother, Alfred Daniel; sister, Christine; and Martin Jr.

through the Emancipation Proclamation of 1863 and the Thirteenth Amendment at the end of the Civil War (1861–1865). But the end of slavery had not ended racial prejudice.

Segregation through Jim Crow laws dominated the South in the 1930s. The laws separated people based on the color of their skin in places such as restaurants, hospitals, and schools. Black and white people couldn't drink from the same water fountains or use the same bathrooms. They couldn't sit together on buses and trains. A Georgia law even dictated whom white people could marry: "It shall be unlawful for a white person to marry anyone except a white person." Under Jim Crow laws, services such as medical care were usually inferior for black people, if the services existed at all.

Martin soon experienced prejudice firsthand. At a shoe store in Atlanta, a clerk refused to serve Martin and his father because they were sitting in seats reserved for white

A segregated drinking fountain in Halifax, North Carolina, in 1938

Passengers wait in a segregated section of the Durham, North Carolina, bus station.

people. Martin and other black people couldn't go to public parks, some restaurants, and most swimming pools and movie theaters.

A white family owned a store across the street from Martin's home, and their son spent a lot of time at the store. He was the same age as Martin, and the two boys became friends and played together often. At the age of six, they were old enough to begin school, but Jim Crow laws forced them to attend separate schools. Soon Martin's friend told him that they couldn't play together anymore. Martin was stunned and upset. Martin's parents had taught him that it was his duty as a Christian to love others, including white people. But he wondered how he could love people who treated him differently because of the color of his skin.

BRIGHT STUDENT

From 1941 to 1945, millions of men and women left their jobs and schools in the United States to fight in World War II (1939–1945). This left fewer college-age students at home in the United States, so Atlanta's Morehouse College began accepting younger students. Martin excelled in high school and took Morehouse's entrance exam in 1944. He passed and became a college student at the age of fifteen.

Martin Luther King Jr. (*front row, third from left*) listens to a speaker during an assembly at Morehouse College in 1948.

Martin's father and grandfather had attended Morehouse, and both had become pastors after graduation. Walter McCall, Martin's close college friend, felt certain he wanted to become a pastor. Martin wasn't as certain of his own future. He wanted to serve

Benjamin E. Mays (*left*) helped inspire King to become an activist.

society too. But in his first years at Morehouse, he studied law and medicine. He thought he could help more people as a doctor or a lawyer than he could in a church.

Morehouse's president, Benjamin E. Mays, became an important figure in Martin's life. Mays was a minister who taught that it wasn't enough to be "sensitive to the wrongs, the sufferings and the injustices of society." People must also "accept responsibility for correcting these ills." The message helped spark Martin's interest in racial justice—he was ready to take action to correct the problems he saw in society.

At Morehouse, Martin began to form ideas about how he could take action. He read the essay "Civil Disobedience" by Henry David Thoreau and learned about using nonviolent methods to protest unjust laws. The idea of refusing to cooperate with an unjust system such as Jim Crow laws appealed to Martin. By his final year at Morehouse, he had decided to follow his father's path and become a pastor. The lessons of Mays helped Martin see that religious leaders could fight for social justice. Martin graduated from Morehouse in 1948 at the age of nineteen.

HENRY DAVID THOREAU

Born on July 12, 1817, Henry David Thoreau spent most of his life in Concord, Massachusetts. He attended Harvard University and began a brief teaching career after graduation. With his friend Ralph Waldo Emerson, Thoreau became a leading writer and thinker in a philosophy that focused on the spiritual rather than the material world.

Thoreau strongly opposed slavery and the Mexican-American War (1846–1848), a fight over territory in what would become the southwestern United States. To avoid supporting the war and US slavery, he stopped paying taxes. In 1846 Thoreau was arrested for tax evasion, and he spent a night in jail. He was released after someone else paid his taxes. The experience inspired him to write "Civil Disobedience," in which he argued that a citizen has the right to break laws to protest an unjust government. "Under a government which imprisons any unjustly," Thoreau wrote, "the true place for a just man is also a prison."

That year King enrolled at Crozer Theological Seminary near Philadelphia, Pennsylvania, to begin his formal religious education. At Crozer, King read many books and studied the ideas of many great thinkers, especially the ideas of Mohandas Gandhi.

Gandhi was born in India in 1869. India was a British colony then, and early in the twentieth century, Gandhi led a nonviolent resistance movement against British control of his country. The movement included hunger strikes and worker walkouts. Under Gandhi's leadership, India gained independence from Britain in 1947. The peaceful Indian leader was assassinated in 1948.

Mohandas Gandhi

In 1950 King traveled to Philadelphia to hear a sermon by Pastor Mordecai Johnson, who had just returned from a trip to India, where he met with people in Gandhi's movement. Johnson spoke of Gandhi and the movement against Britain, and King was impressed. He set out to learn everything he could about Gandhi and his nonviolent methods.

King graduated from Crozer in 1951. Yet he still

wasn't finished with school. That year he started classes at the School of Theology at Boston University to earn a doctorate degree. In Boston he also met someone who would change his life forever: Coretta Scott. The two went on their first date, lunch, in January of 1952. Over the next few months, they began a romantic relationship, and in November, Martin told his family he planned to marry Coretta. Seventeen months after they met, the couple took their vows.

LEADING A MOVEMENT

By 1953 King had finished most of his work at Boston University. With school nearly behind him, a world of possibilities became available. He had long thought

Martin Luther King Jr. and Coretta Scott King in Montgomery, Alabama, in 1956

about becoming a teacher, and he received job offers from several schools and churches that needed a pastor. He and his new wife, Coretta Scott King, decided that they could best serve people in the South, where Jim Crow laws continued to oppress black people. In 1954 King became the pastor at Dexter Avenue Baptist Church in Montgomery, Alabama.

CORETTA SCOTT

Coretta Scott was born in 1927 and grew up in central Alabama. It was a time and place where racial divides ran deep. Like all African Americans in Alabama then, the Scott family experienced racial prejudice and violence. Coretta thrived in school and attended Antioch College in Yellow Springs, Ohio. There she joined groups such as the National Association for the Advancement of Colored People (NAACP), which promoted racial and social justice. When she met King in Boston in 1952, part of her attraction to the serious young man was his dedication to social justice. On June 18, 1953, Martin Luther King Sr. oversaw the wedding of his son and Coretta Scott on the lawn of the Scott's home in Alabama. Between 1955 and 1963, the couple had four children: Yolanda, Martin III, Dexter, and Bernice.

In 1955 King received his degree and officially became Dr. Martin Luther King Jr. That was just the beginning of what would be a huge year in King's life. On November 17, his first child, Yolanda, was born. About two weeks later, a black activist named Rosa Parks refused to give up her seat to a white passenger on a Montgomery city bus, setting off a series of events that would launch a movement and put King in the national spotlight.

On December 1, Parks took the bus home from her job at a Montgomery department store. She sat in the

A police photo of Rosa Parks after her arrest in December 1955

rear section of the bus, where black people were expected to sit. Soon the white section of the bus filled with passengers, and the bus driver told Parks to give up her seat so a white person could sit there. The moment was a turning point in her life and in US history. "I had been pushed around all my life and felt at this moment that I couldn't take it anymore," Parks wrote. She refused to move, and the police arrested her.

The black community of Montgomery jumped into action. The next day, King's phone rang early in the morning. E. D. Nixon, a community leader, was on the line. He told King about Parks's arrest and explained a plan to boycott city buses in Montgomery. Jo Ann Robinson was a member of the Women's Political Council, a group working to improve the lives of black people in Montgomery. Overnight, she and a few others had passed out more than fifty thousand fliers calling for a boycott of city buses on December 5. The flier pleaded with the black community to take action. "If you do not do something to stop those arrests, they will continue," it stated. "The next time it may be you, or your daughter or your mother."

On the day of the boycott, King and his wife awoke early and watched the street in front of their home. Soon a bus that was usually full of black riders drove by. It was empty. Then two more empty buses passed. The boycott was working! After driving around the city and seeing black people everywhere walking to work, King headed to the courthouse for Parks's trial. She was found guilty of violating segregation laws and fined ten dollars, plus four dollars for court costs.

Later that day, King headed to a meeting where Nixon, another Montgomery pastor named Ralph Abernathy, and other community leaders discussed their next move. They decided to form the Montgomery Improvement Association. In minutes King was nominated and

During the Montgomery bus boycott, huge numbers of African Americans walked to work instead of taking buses.

Rosa Parks and a reporter pose for photos on a bus in 1956, after the successful bus boycott.

approved as the group's new president. He hadn't even had time to decide whether he wanted the job.

At 7:00 p.m. on December 5, the Montgomery Improvement Association held a public rally at Holt Street Baptist Church. As president, King addressed the crowd. He was nervous. Public speaking came naturally to him as a pastor, but this was different. Things had happened so quickly that day that King hadn't had time to prepare a speech. He had no idea how many people would show up to the rally, and he didn't know if they would be open to his message. King wanted to encourage the community to continue the boycott and fight for racial justice. But he didn't want them to turn to hatred or violence. The young leader was determined to promote social change with unity and love.

As he approached the church with an outline of a speech in his mind, King was shocked by the number of people he saw. Thousands of community members filled the building. The sight gave him hope that the boycott would continue. TV cameras and audio recorders captured King's speech. He told the story of Rosa Parks's arrest and spoke of the long history of abuse black people had suffered in Montgomery. He said that it was time to demand respect. He also called for unity and kindness in their struggle, and a loving spirit toward their fellow humans.

The crowd stood and clapped as the speech ended. King was pleased that the people had accepted his message. As the applause faded, Abernathy walked to the speaking platform. He and a small group of association members had been working on a list of changes they wanted to see on Montgomery buses. Abernathy was ready to present the list to the larger group for their approval. Abernathy's list called for a guarantee that Montgomery city bus drivers treat everyone with respect. It required that bus rules change to allow any passenger to take

King speaks to community members at a rally during the Montgomery bus boycott.

an open seat and not be forced to give up the seat to someone else. And it demanded that black drivers be assigned to bus routes that went through mostly black neighborhoods to help ensure that riders be treated respectfully.

Abernathy's resolution stated that the black community of Montgomery wouldn't ride city buses again until the city made the changes they asked for. When he finished reading the list, he asked the crowd if they were in favor of those demands. The people rose to their feet and cheered. The movement for equality was growing.

King works with a group of organizers, including Abernathy (*far left*) and Parks (*front center*), on the bus boycott.

FIGHTING WITH LOVE

Montgomery buses lost 90 percent of their passengers on the first day of the boycott. To keep it going, King and the association raised money for carpools to get people to work. As days passed and the boycott continued, city officials tried to stop it. The city was losing money because so few people were riding buses. The mayor criticized the movement on TV. The police began to harass carpool drivers to try to break their spirits, and they questioned and arrested association members.

During the boycott, King became a target for police and city officials who disagreed with him, but he never lost sight of his goals.

In January 1956, the police followed King as he was driving a few other people home. The police knew King was one of the leaders of the boycott. King made sure to drive carefully, but the police arrested him for speeding. He spent part of the day in jail, and the experience made him even more determined to work for justice. He continued to push his message that lasting change could come only through peaceful protest. He told association members that no matter how often they were arrested, they should continue to respond with love.

Some in Montgomery responded to King's message of

love with violence. At 9:30 p.m. on January 30, while King was at a meeting at First Baptist Church, his wife was at home visiting with a friend when they heard a thump and a boom. A bomb had exploded on the front porch. King rushed home. No one was hurt.

Arrests and bombings frightened the black community of Montgomery, but the activists stayed determined in the face of violence. The boycott continued. Meanwhile, association member Fred Gray prepared a lawsuit challenging the segregation of Montgomery buses. By the end of 1956, the case had reached the US Supreme Court. On November 13, the court ruled that bus segregation was illegal, and the ruling went into effect on December 20. King declared an end to the boycott after 381 days,

Other activists faced violence too. Abernathy (*right*) and the Reverend W. J. Hudson survey the scene after a bomb exploded at Abernathy's house.

and on December 21, he boarded a Montgomery bus with Nixon, Abernathy, and others.

People around the country heard about the success of the boycott. Much of the attention fell on King as head of the movement. King, Abernathy, and other Montgomery Improvement Association leaders held a series of meetings in Atlanta and New Orleans, Louisiana, in January and February 1957. They formed the Southern Christian Leadership Conference. The leaders wanted

King stands near a bus at the end of the Montgomery bus boycott on December 26, 1956.

to capitalize on the momentum of the victory in Montgomery by planning peaceful civil rights protests and encouraging black people to vote across the South. The new group chose King as president. Also in February, he appeared on the cover of *Time* magazine. The article described him as a leader of black people throughout the South in the fight to end segregation.

The following year, on September 17, 1958, King released his book, *Stride toward Freedom: The Montgomery Story.* At a book signing in New York a few days later, a woman approached his table. She asked if he was Martin Luther King. When he said yes, the woman stabbed King in the chest with a 7-inch (18 cm) letter opener. Doctors removed the blade and saved his life.

INSPIRED TO RESIST

By February 1959, King had recovered from his chest wound and was able to fly with his wife to India to trace the path of one of his heroes. The teachings of Gandhi had inspired King throughout the Montgomery bus boycott. King was eager to visit the country where Gandhi had lived and developed his message of nonviolent resistance. King spoke with Indian leaders and visited poor and wealthy areas of the country. He found that people welcomed him warmly, and he saw that the country had done a better job of integrating people of different classes and races than the United States had. Seeing the success of Gandhi's peaceful resistance movement in India reinforced King's belief that nonviolence was the only way to reach lasting equality for black people in the United States.

In 1960 King and his family moved to Atlanta to be closer to the Southern Christian Leadership Conference headquarters there. He also became co-pastor of Ebenezer Baptist Church with his father. Around then a movement of student sit-ins spread in

Coretta Scott King (*left*) and Martin Luther King Jr. arrive at the airport in New Delhi, India, in 1959.

Protesters stage a sit-in at a lunch counter in Greensboro, North Carolina, after workers refused to serve them.

the South. Young black people sat down at places such as segregated lunch counters that were reserved for white people and refused to leave. Sometimes the protest ended peacefully. Other times the protesters were beaten, arrested, or both. But they followed the teachings of King and Gandhi and didn't strike back with violence. Student activists such as John Lewis formed the Student Nonviolent Coordinating Committee to organize sit-ins and other protests against racial injustice.

King took part in a sit-in at a department store in Atlanta on October 19, 1960. The police arrested him, and he spent about a week in jail. Before that, he had never spent more than a few hours behind bars.

The Congress of Racial Equality was pushing for civil rights for black people. Joining with groups such as the Student Nonviolent Coordinating Committee, the groups

King meets with a group of college activists to plan strategies for the 1960 lunch counter sit-ins.

began what would be known as Freedom Rides. Black and white riders boarded two buses on May 4, 1961, and left Washington, DC, on a trip through the South to protest bus segregation in the region. The riders faced angry protesters throughout the trip. In South Carolina, John Lewis and another rider were beaten. King met with the riders in Atlanta and warned them about Alabama. He was concerned that the trip would end violently in his former state.

King was right. In Alabama, protesters threw a firebomb onto one of the buses, forcing the riders to flee for their lives. Another Freedom Ride a few days later ended with beatings in Montgomery. King held a rally at the city's First Baptist Church to plead for bloodshed to end. An angry mob appeared outside. The National Guard escorted people out of the church to avoid more hostility. The violence and the presence of the National Guard brought national attention to the Freedom Rides, and King was viewed as a leader of the campaign.

King used his growing status to bring more attention to civil rights protests in other segregated cities. In December 1961, the police in Albany, Georgia, arrested King at demonstrations there. With no promises from the city to eliminate segregation, protests restarted in July 1962. The police arrested him again. This time, a

Freedom Riders Julia Aaron and David Dennis are escorted by members of the National Guard on a bus from Montgomery, Alabama, to Jackson, Mississippi.

judge sentenced him to forty-five days in jail, but he was released after just a few days.

The protests in Albany did not bring about the results King was hoping for, but King learned from the experience. He realized the protests in Albany had not focused on a specific goal. King used these lessons as he prepared for more effective demonstrations in other cities, including Birmingham, Alabama. To prevent protests, Birmingham officials obtained a court order saying that protesters needed a permit. On April 12, 1963, King led hundreds of black protesters on a march in defiance of that order. The police arrested King, Abernathy, and other marchers, and they spent about a week in jail.

While King was in jail, eight white Jewish and Christian leaders published a letter in the *Birmingham News*. The letter stated that the legal system was the proper place to fight against segregation, and it called for people to withdraw their support from the protests. The

A group of National Guardsmen wait for a Freedom Riders bus in 1961.

Birmingham police arrest King (*right*) and Abernathy (*left*) at an April 12, 1963, protest.

message upset King. In his jail cell, he wrote on the edges of newspapers and other scraps of paper to respond to the letter. He pointed out Birmingham's long history of bias and the slow pace of positive change. And he explained why black people were willing to break the law to achieve justice—if they didn't demand change, they would never get it.

MARCHING FOR JUSTICE

Newspapers across the country published King's "Letter from Birmingham Jail" in 1963, adding to his reputation as a national voice for freedom. That summer when he attended the March on Washington for Jobs and Freedom, he was widely considered the face of the civil rights movement. The event—and especially King's stirring speech—made him even better known as an important civil rights leader in the United States.

Time magazine named him Man of the Year for 1963. The honor reflected the impact that King and the civil rights movement had had on the nation. In 1963 President John F. Kennedy announced that he would encourage Congress to pass new laws to end segregation in public places. "This nation, for all its hopes and all its boasts, will not be fully free until all its citizens are free," Kennedy said.

Kennedy was assassinated in November 1963. But his death didn't stop the push for civil rights laws. His successor, Lyndon B. Johnson, took up the cause. On July 2, 1964, Johnson signed the Civil Rights Act. King, Lewis, and other civil rights leaders stood nearby. The

President Lyndon B. Johnson signs the 1964 Civil Rights Act. King looks on from behind.

act banned discrimination in the United States in public places and places of employment. The law was a huge step toward racial justice for black people in the United States.

King's success in achieving nonviolent social change earned him the 1964 Nobel Peace Prize. The prize came with an award of about $54,000, and King said he would donate all of it to the civil rights movement. He knew that despite recent successes, the struggle for equal rights was far from finished.

The Civil Rights Act didn't end voter discrimination—people against civil rights still found plenty of ways to prevent black people from voting. They made it difficult for black people to register to vote by forcing them to take reading tests. Election officials would tell potential voters they had failed the tests. Officials might also find small mistakes on voter registration forms and say these mistakes disqualified people from voting. If complex forms and tests didn't work, some used physical intimidation to keep black people from the polls. To bring attention to the issue, the Southern Christian Leadership Conference organized a march. Lewis planned to lead hundreds of people from Selma, Alabama, to Montgomery on March 7, 1965. But before they even left Selma, police attacked the marchers with clubs and teargas on the Edmund Pettus Bridge. The police forced the marchers back into the city. Reporters on the scene captured images of the violence. The images appeared on TVs and newspapers across the country.

King led another march two days later. Again, police

Civil rights marchers walk back toward Selma on March 7, 1965, after police attacked them on the bridge and forced them to turn around.

blocked the marchers on the bridge. This time, the protesters stopped and prayed, and the police let them pass. Instead of continuing to Montgomery, though, King turned the group back toward Selma. Some people called his decision cowardly, but he believed he had proven his point that peace was the only way forward.

On March 21, about two thousand protesters again set out from Selma. This time, Johnson sent US Army and National Guard troops to protect the protesters. The marchers arrived in Montgomery on March 25, and more than twenty-five thousand people gathered in front of the state capitol. King spoke to the crowd, promising them that soon black people would be free of voter discrimination.

During the events in Selma and Montgomery, Johnson asked Congress to create laws that would prevent voter discrimination. King was at the White

House on August 6, 1965, when the president signed the Voting Rights Act. It ensured the right to vote for black people and outlawed many of the practices that kept them from the polls. Voter turnout surged among black people in some parts of the South.

A LIFE OF SERVICE

The success of the civil rights movement in the South inspired King to keep working for social justice in other areas as well. In 1966 King and his family moved to Chicago. It was part of the Southern Christian Leadership Conference's plan to protest the slums—poor neighborhoods filled with run-down homes and violent gang activity—where black people often had to live. King's presence in

King accepts the Nobel Peace Prize in Norway in December 1964.

these slums brought attention to the issue, and he led several marches to fight for better living and working conditions for black people in the city. The actions represented the conference's first activities in a northern city.

On December 4, 1967, King announced the Poor People's Campaign. King and other civil rights leaders planned to organize a march in Washington, DC, the following spring to demand help for the poorest Americans. But first, he was needed in Memphis, Tennessee. City workers there were on strike to protest discrimination and unfair working conditions, and one of the organizers called King for help.

King went to Memphis in March 1968 to support the strike, but a march turned into a riot, and the police arrested hundreds of protesters. King returned to Memphis the next month with the intention of holding a peaceful march. On April 3, he gave a speech to city workers and supporters. The next evening, he stepped onto his hotel balcony, and an assassin shot him. King fell and was pronounced dead an hour later. James Earl Ray, a well-known criminal and longtime racist, was arrested for King's murder on June 8.

Widespread mourning by people of all races followed the news of King's death. In the years to come, people honored him and the movement he led. In 1983 Congress made King's birthday a national holiday. A few years later, the National Civil Rights Museum opened where the Lorraine Motel, the site of King's murder, once stood. The Martin Luther King Jr. Memorial—on the National Mall between the Lincoln Memorial and the Thomas Jefferson Memorial—opened in 2011. Standing at the base of the statue of King at a ceremony dedicating the memorial, President Barack Obama reminded the crowd that despite's King's great deeds, the civil rights leader's work still wasn't finished. The United States continues to struggle with discrimination and inequality between people of different races, genders, and economic backgrounds. Many people continue to hold protests and fight against this inequality and other issues such as gun violence, abuse, and the unjust treatment of immigrants. These people follow in King's path, and despite the ongoing problems in society, Obama had hope for the future. "I know we will overcome," Obama said. "I know there are better days ahead. I know this because of the man towering over us."

Americans continue to work toward King's dreams and honor his legacy more than fifty years after his death.

IMPORTANT DATES

1929   Martin Luther King Jr. is born on January 15 in Atlanta, Georgia.

1944   He passes the Morehouse College entrance exam and becomes a college student.

1948   He begins his studies at Crozer Theological Seminary.

1951   He graduates from Crozer at the top of his class and begins classes at the School of Theology at Boston University.

1955   The Montgomery bus boycott begins, and King becomes the movement's leader.

1956   A bomb explodes on the front porch of King's home in Montgomery, Alabama. His wife and daughter Yolanda are home, but no one is hurt.

        The US Supreme Court rules that segregation on Montgomery buses is illegal, and King ends the boycott on December 21.

1957   King becomes president of the newly formed Southern Christian Leadership Conference in Atlanta.

1958	He survives a stab wound in the chest with a letter opener at a book signing in New York.
1960	King and his family move to Atlanta, where he becomes co-pastor with his father at Ebenezer Baptist Church.
1961	Freedom Rides in the South end in violence.
1963	King publishes "Letter from Birmingham Jail," bringing more national attention to the struggle for civil rights and raising his status as a leader of the movement.
	King delivers a rousing speech at the March on Washington for Jobs and Freedom.
1964	President Johnson signs the Civil Rights Act.
1965	Johnson signs the Voting Rights Act.
1968	King is killed on his hotel balcony in Memphis, Tennessee.
2011	The Martin Luther King Jr. Memorial opens on the National Mall in Washington, DC.

SOURCE NOTES

11 Michiko Kakutani, "The Lasting Power of Dr. King's Dream Speech," *New York Times*, August 27, 2013, https://www .nytimes.com/2013/08/28/us/the-lasting-power-of-dr-kings -dream-speech.html.

14 "Jim Crow Laws," National Park Service, accessed May 6, 2018, https://www.nps.gov/malu/learn/education/jim_crow_laws.htm.

17 "King at Morehouse," Morehouse College, accessed May 13, 2018, http://www.morehouse.edu/kingcollection/life.php.

18 "Thoreau and 'Civil Disobedience,'" Constitutional Rights Foundation, accessed May 19, 2018, http://www.crf-usa.org /black-history-month/thoreau-and-civil-disobedience.

22 Jeanne Theoharis, "How History Got the Rosa Parks Story Wrong," *Washington Post*, December 1, 2015, https://www .washingtonpost.com/posteverything/wp/2015/12/01/how -history-got-the-rosa-parks-story-wrong/?utm_term= .b7d4544f406a.

22 "Rosa Parks Chronology," Smithsonian Source, accessed May 20, 2018, http://www.smithsoniansource.org/display/primarysource /viewdetails.aspx?PrimarySourceId=1203.

36 "John F. Kennedy Speeches: Radio and Television Report to the American People on Civil Rights, June 11, 1963," John F. Kennedy Presidential Library and Museum, accessed May 22, 2018, https://www.jfklibrary.org/Research/Research-Aids/JFK -Speeches/Civil-Rights-Radio-and-Television-Report_19630611 .aspx.

41 "Americans Urged to Live MLK's Ideals at Memorial Dedication," *CNN*, October 17, 2011, https://www.cnn.com/2011/10/16/us/mlk -memorial/index.html.

SELECTED BIBLIOGRAPHY

"Civil Rights Act (1964)." Our Documents. Accessed May 24, 2018. https://www.ourdocuments.gov/doc.php?flash=true&doc=97.

"'I Have a Dream,' Address Delivered at the March on Washington for Jobs and Freedom." Martin Luther King, Jr. Research and Education Institute. Accessed April 21, 2018. https://kinginstitute.stanford.edu /king-papers/documents/i-have-dream-address-delivered-march -washington-jobs-and-freedom.

King, Martin Luther, Jr. *The Autobiography of Martin Luther King, Jr.* New York: Warner Books, 1998.

King, Martin Luther, Jr. *Stride toward Freedom: The Montgomery Story.* Boston: Beacon, 2010.

"March on Washington for Jobs and Freedom." National Park Service. Accessed April 21, 2018. https://www.nps.gov/articles/march-on -washington.htm.

"Martin Luther King Jr.–Biography." Nobelprize.org. Accessed May 24, 2018. https://www.nobelprize.org/nobel_prizes/peace/laureates/1964 /king-bio.html.

FURTHER READING

BOOKS

Braun, Eric. *Taking Action for Civil and Political Rights.* Minneapolis: Lerner Publications, 2017. Learn about some of the ways activists fight for the rights of others and how you can too.

Doeden, Matt. *John Lewis: Courage in Action.* Minneapolis: Lerner Publications, 2018. Read about John Lewis, a civil rights leader who was inspired by Martin Luther King Jr. and later became a member of the US Congress.

Outcalt, Todd. *All about Martin Luther King, Jr.* Indianapolis: Blue River, 2016. Find out more about the leader of the civil rights movement in this illustrated biography.

WEBSITES

Civil Rights Movement
> https://www.jfklibrary.org/JFK/JFK-in-History/Civil-Rights
> -Movement.aspx
> Learn more about the civil rights movement and the people who
> fought for justice in the United States.

The King Center
> http://www.thekingcenter.org/
> Coretta Scott King started the King Center in honor of her husband's
> legacy. Read about the center, and learn more about King's life and
> work.

Martin Luther King, Jr. Memorial
> https://www.nps.gov/mlkm/index.htm
> Check out images and read information about the Martin Luther
> King, Jr. Memorial in Washington, DC.

INDEX